SPACE
SYSTEMS

Gravity, Orbiting Objects, and Planetary Motion

Lisa Hiton

Cavendish
Square

New York

Published in 2017 by Cavendish Square Publishing, LLC
243 5th Avenue, Suite 136, New York, NY 10016

Library of Congress Cataloging-in-Publication Data

Names: Hiton, Lisa, author.
Title: Gravity, orbiting objects, and planetary motion / Lisa Hiton.
Description: New York : Cavendish Square Publishing, [2017] | Series: Space systems | Includes bibliographical references and index.
Identifiers: LCCN 2016025937 (print) | LCCN 2016027929 (ebook) | ISBN 9781502622877 (library bound) | ISBN 9781502622884 (ebook)
Subjects: LCSH: Gravity--Juvenile literature. | Planets--Orbits--Juvenile literature. | Kepler's laws--Juvenile literature.
Classification: LCC QC178 .H56 2017 (print) | LCC QC178 (ebook) | DDC 531.14--dc23

LC record available at https://lccn.loc.gov/2016025937

Editorial Director: David McNamara
Editor: Caitlyn Miller
Copy Editor: Rebecca Rohan
Associate Art Director: Amy Greenan
Designer: Alan Sliwinski
Production Coordinator: Karol Szymczuk
Photo Research: J8 Media

The photographs in this book are used by permission and through the courtesy of: Cover BSIP/UIG/Getty Images; p. 4 Babak Tafreshi/Getty Images; p. 8 Oorka/Shutterstock.com; p. 10 Heritage Images/Hulton Archive/Getty Images; p. 13 Public Domain/File:Flammarion.jpg/Wikimedia Commons; p. 15 British Library/File:THE ILLIAD OF HOMER (translated by POPE)p5.171 The Shield of Achilles.jpg/Wikimedia Commons; p. 17 Public Doman/Bibi Saint-Pol/File:Anaximander world map-en.svg/Wikimedia Commons; p. 24 Panos Karas/Shutterstock.com; p. 26 Print Collector/Hulton Archive/Getty Images; p. 30 Ron Miller/Stocktrek Images/Getty Images; p. 33 Herbert Hall Turner/File:Voyage in Space page023.png/Wikimedia Commons; p. 42 Dorling Kindersley/Getty Images; p. 46 Koya979/Shutterstock.com; p. 48 Wellcome Images/File:Portrait of Nicolas Copernicus Wellcome M0006157.jpg/Wikimedia Commons; p. 52 ullstein bild/Getty Images; p. 55 Nicku/Shutterstock.com; p. 59 Anefo/File:Albert Einstein (portret).jpg/Wikimedia Commons; p. 62 Bryan Bedder/Getty Images for Breakthrough Prize Foundation; p. 68 NASA, ESA, HEIC and The Hubble Heritage Team, STSci/AURA©; p. 74 NASA/File:Hubble Space Telescope.jpg/Wikimedia Commons; p. 77 Bettmann/Getty Images; p. 79, 81 NASA; p. 82 O. Louis Mazzatenta/Getty Images; p. 84 NASA/File:GPS Satellite NASA art-iif.jpg/Wikimedia Commons; p. 92 Mark Garlick/SPL/Getty Images; p. 95 Encyclopaedia Britannica/UIG/Getty Images; p. 96 NASA, ESA, and the Hubble Heritage (STScI/AURA)ESA/Hubble Collaboration; p. 98 NASA/WMAP Science Team/File:CMB Timeline300 no WMAP. jpg/Wikimedia Commons; p. 101 Coldcreation/File:Lambda-Cold Dark Matter, Accelerated Expansion of the Universe, Big Bang-Inflation.jpg/Wikimedia Commons.

Printed in the United States of America

Contents

Betelgeuse

Orion

Rigel

Orion
Nebula

Rosette
Nebula

Monoceros

Lepus

Sirius

Canis Major

Before the telescope, astronomers studied what they could see with the naked eye and named constellations.

Introduction: Our Mysterious Universe

Humans have been curious about the night sky since the dawn of time. When Earth turns away from the sun, the constellations loom over us. At certain moments, they seem mythic: they are part of our storytelling. We look to them and see shapes of characters. We look to them and see maps we've followed to navigate back home. At other times, a look toward the cosmos seems overbearing—mysterious in its stillness and distance, so unlike the fluffy clouds we see during the day.

Our ancestors had fewer means of figuring out the night sky than we do today. Without being able to take photographs, use a **telescope**, or leave Earth, ancient models of planetary motion had little grounding in scientific truth. Astronomy and astrology were still linked together. The mythology and the math were in constant dialogue, helping scientists and the masses fill in the blanks of existence. Everything that was believed had to be seen with the naked eye. And what was missing was filled in by mystic and religious ideas.

From these ancient times, people believed that Earth was flat and that the sun and moon revolved around it each day. Because we grow up with images of Earth and the rest of our solar system from outer space, it seems ridiculous now that people believed those visions to be scientifically true. Yet prevailing beliefs encouraged people to maintain this understanding, without the constant inquiry and proof needed in science.

By the Middle Ages, the tension between the Catholic Church and the sciences was growing stronger. A few brave men during the Scientific Revolution dared to advance science despite censorship. Plus, as modernity loomed, humans invented more instruments of observation and measurement for their cause. Perhaps the most iconic machine in understanding planetary motion is Galileo's telescope. Though we've enhanced the telescope's abilities, we still use this invention to observe the universe today.

With the planets clearly before man's eye, it became harder to deny the truth—that Earth was not central, but was in fact orbiting around the sun. This new way of understanding planetary motion led to political consequences for scientists, but also to many discoveries and advancements in the sciences. Major figures made developments in scientific methods and thinking, innovated and refined a myriad of scientific inventions, and created art to reflect the struggles and triumphs of the time. After Galileo's death, the scientific truths of planetary motion became less controversial. This environment led to the grand synthesis of physics by one man, Sir Isaac Newton.

As in the mythic figures in the sky, the legend of Newton began where creation in the Old Testament began: at an apple tree. An apple fell, and the young Newton wondered, *Why does an apple always fall to the ground in this fashion?* With Newton's question came an answer that would shake the world entirely: **gravity**. While scientists before were able to describe motion, none could explain why things moved. Newton's description of gravity as a universal force summoned waves of intellectual inquiry and scientific advancement across many fields of science. Further, it helped us understand our daily lives.

The world would be at peace with these ideas and advancements for hundreds of years. In fact, most of the physics we encounter on Earth still follows the ideals of Newton. But at the turn of the twentieth century, everything in the world began to change.

Radium. Airplanes. X-rays. Radio. Machine guns. These were some of the many inventions that changed the world at the turn of the century. While scientists and inventors were

Though there's no way to observe black holes yet, scientists understand the effect of black holes through the behavior of nearby matter.

constantly on the brink of discovery and advancement, the tone of these achievements became a war cry. The urgency to discover was a product of two world wars. And amidst the violence rose one genius, Albert Einstein.

Because so much had been discovered in optics, magnetism, and quantum mechanics, some of Newton's ideas weren't holding true to the behaviors of subatomic particles or large bodies in space. Einstein presented his ideas of **relativity** to the world. His unique means of discovery, complex thought-experiments, prevailed. From winning the Nobel Prize to helping build the atomic bomb, Einstein's ideas were tested and proven over and over in small and large ways. To this day, his ideas hold true.

Though Einstein is gone, his work continues to affect our daily lives. From GPS on our phones to the recent discovery of **gravitational waves**, Einstein's laws of physics have yet to be disproven. Since Einstein's time we've landed on the moon and proven that black holes exist. His work has paved the way for cosmologists to figure out the **big bang** and other qualities of the universe's origins. It is in this moment that humans are back in a place of exploration.

We've gone from a population uncertain of what was out there to one that sees our own solar system clearly. And though the ideas of our ancestors past seem simple now, someday, our ideas about the big bang will be proven right or wrong, and all of our predictions may seem simple to humans of the future. It is this endless cycle of inquiry and observation that keeps science alive.

The circular map on this clay tablet is
numbered and labeled in cuneiform script.
The two outer circles represent water.

Early
Predictions

G ravity. It's a force that we often take for granted. Every time we take a step and stay on Earth, we have gravity to thank. Like breathing, gravity is part of our involuntary state of being. But humans have only known about and understood gravity since the 1600s.

Our understanding of Earth began with the naked eye. The ideas of early peoples with regard to planetary motion consisted of what we still can see today. When we walk around, it's not obvious that Earth is a sphere. It seems that things are level and flat. Further, in a time before airplanes and trains, travel was limited to being on foot or being on a boat. The mysteries of the edge of the Earth occupied the minds of early humans the way the edges of the universe are at the forefront of astronomy today.

EARLY PREDICTIONS

Before the digital age, our understanding of nature and the cosmos came primarily from observation. Observation is still a central element to the scientific process, but nowadays, we can prove or disprove our predications with rapid speed using various technologies. One of the oldest myths about Earth, for many centuries, was that it was flat. It's difficult to imagine believing that now—we have digital mapping, photos from outer space, and lots of scientific discovery to prove that Earth is a sphere, how and why we have seasons, and where our planet is in relation to the sun and other planets. But in a time before photography and other technology, it was difficult to understand Earth as anything but flat. Another larger misunderstanding was that Earth was the center of the universe.

FLAT EARTH

Many societies believed that Earth was flat through ancient times. To this day, we have many emblems of this flat Earth **cosmography**, or maps of heaven and Earth that support the flat Earth theories and beliefs of different cultures.

Flat Earth of the Ancient Near East

The first place to look for these old theories of the cosmos is in the oldest-known civilizations. In Egypt, Earth was depicted as a flat disk floating in a large body of water. The

Named for Camille Flammarion, this 1888 wood engraving was paired with Flammarion's book, *The Atmosphere: Popular Meteorology.*

ancient Egyptian pyramid texts and coffin texts also describe flat landmasses (like islands) floating in one large ocean. The pyramid texts are a collection of spells meant to protect a pharaoh's remains and help him ascend to heaven in the afterlife. Coffin texts were funeral spells for royalty as well.

Similarly, the Israelites depicted Earth this way, with the addition of the sky as a dividing line that separates Earth from the heavens. One of the oldest and most famous emblems of this version of Earth is the Flammarion engraving. In the image, a man reaches the end of the Earth, kneels down, and pokes his head through the firmament between Earth and heaven.

Another depiction comes from Babylonia (a region of Mesopotamia). This ancient Sumerian culture produced the oldest artifact found so far with a portrayal of Earth. The Imago mundi, or Babylonian Map of the World, is a fifth- or sixth-century clay tablet featuring an image of the world. It currently resides in the British Museum. The diagram shows Babylon in the center of the map, other flat lands floating in water, and a closed river to represent the outer perimeter of the universe.

In many of these cases, the link between religion, the afterlife, and the cosmos is no coincidence. In the absence of scientific developments and technologies, communities were left with storytelling and mythology to fill in the blanks about these large forces.

The Flat Earth of Ancient Greece and Rome

One of the most famous flat Earth sources studied today is the Shield of Achilles. In Homer's epic story, the *Iliad*, Achilles uses a shield to fight Hector. Here is Alexander Pope's translation of some of the lines:

> *Then first he form'd the immense and solid shield;*
> *Rich various artifice emblazed the field;*
> *Its utmost verge a threefold circle bound;*
> *A silver chain suspends the massy round;*

Five ample plates the broad expanse compose,
And godlike labours on the surface rose.
There shone the image of the master-mind:
There earth, there heaven, there ocean he design'd;
The unwearied sun, the moon completely round;
The starry lights that heaven's high convex crown'd;
The Pleiads, Hyads, with the northern team;
And great Orion's more refulgent beam;
To which, around the axle of the sky,
The Bear, revolving, points his golden eye,
Still shines exalted on the ethereal plain,
Nor bathes his blazing forehead in the main.

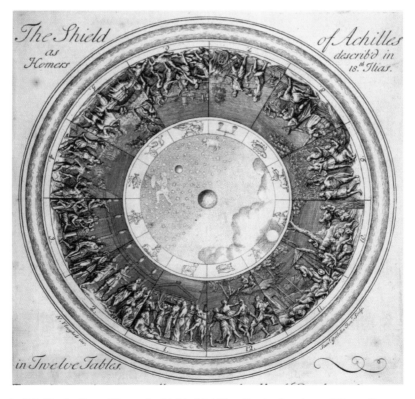

In this illustration of Homer's shield of Achilles, the twelve signs of the zodiac are represented, showing the intertwined beliefs of the mystical and the scientific.

The verse goes on to give even more details that appeared on this mythic shield. The description, in conjunction with many renderings of the shield, serve as the earliest cosmography in Greece's history. One key detail from Homer's version of the universe is the coexistence of the sun and moon. On the shield, they are both shining. In this version, Earth is still encircled by an ocean.

From this epic poem, many Greek philosophers elaborated on the idea of Earth and its potential shape. The term "philosopher" during the time of ancient Greece was a word to describe anyone who loved wisdom. Though nowadays "philosopher" often indicates a specific study of kinds of thinking, early philosophers were also mathematicians, astronomers, and scientists. Before Socrates, many Greek philosophers believed the Earth was flat, and many of them had variations of how this could be true.

Thales of Miletus was known as the first Greek philosopher. In his observations and theories about Earth, everything stemmed from one root: that all of nature originated from water. This explained his theory of the earth-encircling ocean. Unlike Homer's shield and the works of other writers and thinkers, Thales purported these truths without reference to mythology. This effort—to articulate thoughts without use of metaphor or myth—still prevails in philosophical thinking today. Thales thought Earth floated like a log. He was supported by other Greek philosophers for quite some time.

There were many other supporters of the **flat Earth theory**, though they each had their own variation on how it was possible. Anaxagoras and Archelaus believed that Earth was flat, but had a depression at the center, which justified varying sunrise and sunset times. In Anaximander's version, "the earth is flat and rides on air; in the same way the sun and the moon and the other heavenly bodies, which are all fiery,

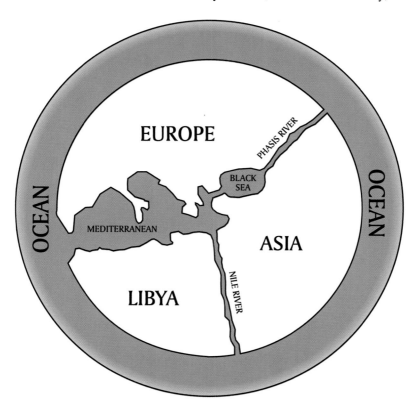

Anaximander's map is thought to be the world's first published map.

The King's Mirror

By the Middle Ages, the Norse belief in flat Earth began to subside. In an old Norse text, *The King's Mirror*, a son and father discuss many matters of general knowledge. In a chapter on the "sun's course," the father describes the relationship between a lighted candle and an apple as a model for the sun in relation to Earth:

If you take a lighted candle and set it in a room, you may expect it to light up the entire interior, unless something should hinder, though the room be quite large. But if you take an apple and hang it close to the flame, so near that it is heated, the apple will darken nearly half the room or even more. However, if you hang the apple near the wall, it will not get hot; the candle will light up the whole house; and the shadow on the wall where the apple hangs will be scarcely half as large as the apple itself. From this you may infer that the earth-circle is round like a ball and not equally near the sun at every point. But where the curved surface lies nearest the sun's path, there will the greatest heat be; and some of the lands that lie continuously under the unbroken rays cannot be inhabited.

In this rendering, the idea that Earth is spherical instead of flat becomes a more common thought. It would take a long time for the world to hold a spherical Earth in the mind as both belief and knowledge.

ride the air because of their flatness." Xenophanes declared Earth was flat, with one side facing the air and the other side extending infinitely.

From scientists to philosophers to poets, the result of all of these ideas was a flat Earth. In ancient texts, the Earth is described as having ends and edges. Even today, our perception of Earth still fits this understanding based on what our eyes and bodies can experience without the help of other technologies and knowledge.

The Flat Earth of the Ancient Germanic Peoples

Norse and Germanic peoples also believed in the flat Earth theory during ancient times. In the Norse creation myth, Earth was surrounded by an ocean. Dwelling in that ocean was a snake called Jormungandr. Within this drawing of the world, there was believed to be an **axis mundi**, or a center pole that connected the geographic and the celestial. Many religions and philosophies reference an axis mundi. In the ancient Norse version, a tree or pillar at the center represents this axis between Earth and the heavens.

The Flat Earth of Ancient India

Like many other views of the time, the Ancient Indian description of Earth also portrayed Earth as flat and surrounded by an ocean. More specifically, the Buddhist cosmography portrayed a round disk with a mountain at the center as Earth. The land was divided into four areas or continents. The flower-like rendering was surrounded by the oceanic disk full of cosmos.

The Flat Earth of Ancient China

In Ancient China, the flat Earth theory depicted a square-shaped Earth and round heavens. Though this may seem farther away, China's most famous astronomers at the time described Earth as being egg-like. Astronomer Zhang Heng described the relationship to the heavens and Earth as: "The heavens are like a hen's egg and round as a crossbow bullet; the earth is like the yolk of the egg, and lies in the center."

The heavens as an egg acknowledged the spherical nature of Earth's movement through the universe. Though whether or not the "square" version of Earth is also meant to describe flatness is up for debate, the intuitive relationship between Earth amongst the cosmos acknowledged some sense of circularity.

GEOCENTRISM

Another early misconception believed by many societies about Earth is that it was the center of the universe. Instead of considering that Earth may revolve around the sun, many felt that Earth (especially in its flat, floating state) was central and the other cosmos floated around it. Even today, it is easy to see how the belief in **geocentrism** could be so strong, especially without other technologies and means of communicating across the world to prove otherwise.

Proof of Spherical Earth

Pythagoras is remembered for first identifying that Earth is spherical. Though others had suggested it before him, his findings were first to dominate public thought in Greece during the sixth century BCE. Pythagoras, like many philosophers before Socrates, was a physicist and mathematician. He was an observer of nature. We remember him mostly for the Pythagorean theorem in geometry. His teachings on numbers are the basis for much of geometry and physics today.

In Pythagoras's astronomical observations, he began to notice and keep track of the moon's shape. The **terminator**—the line dividing the part of the moon in the light from the part in the dark—was not straight as it moved through its cycle each night. For Pythagoras, the moon became a mirror for understanding Earth. If light upon the moon changed based on the moon's roundness, such would have to hold true for Earth.

As with many predictions of both mystic and scientific impulse, many stories came into being around the mystery behind this idea. From famous tales, like the *Odyssey* and the *Iliad*, to fisherman's tales, many people began to notice strange things happening between the Earth, the sea, and the sky. Many told tales of ships disappearing over the horizon. And since many of those ships returned, they couldn't have fallen off of a flat Earth. Many returned from journeys by sea and on foot over great distances, noting that the Pole Star shifted higher in the sky when travelling north.

Aristotle was the first to *prove* that Pythagoras's theory was correct. Astronomers and philosophers took notes and drew diagrams of different solar and lunar eclipses. Aristotle noticed that Earth's shadow on the moon during an eclipse was not elliptical, as in the hypothesized flat-disk-shaped-Earth, but rather, round, as in a sphere. Aristotle also used other mysterious observations to help prove his point. If he looked out to a horizon, the top of an incoming ship's sail would reveal itself before the rest of the ship, complying with his idea of a curved Earth. He even proposed (though vastly underestimated) the first circumference of Earth. And, for those in the community who held tight to more mystic beliefs, Aristotle articulated that Earth was a heavenly body, which meant it was perfect. Since Pythagoras's time, music and the cosmos were very linked. His mathematic explanations for music and sound were already proven and practiced. He promoted the idea that the "divine" in musical harmony was parallel to all things in nature. And so, the perfect sphere of Earth easily fit the beliefs of the time. Aristotle is still known as the "Father of Natural Sciences" for the practices of observation and deduction—the basis of our scientific method today.

Aristotelian Physics

Despite Aristotle's many contributions to thinking and knowledge, he falsely predicted that Earth was the center of the universe. Aristotle's works written in the fourth century BCE were the basis of natural philosophy for more than two thousand years. In Aristotelian physics, Earth is a sphere around which the cosmos spin. In Aristotle's work, two types of motion described the way bodies (like planets) could move: natural motion and violent motion.

Natural motion describes motion that arises from the nature of an object. One of Aristotle's main observations was that heavy objects or bodies fall, naturally, toward the center of Earth. Falling, then, is a natural motion. It's in the object's characteristics to behave in this way. Because of this observation, Aristotle concluded that, for example, heavenly bodies made of ether (the substance he believed filled the universe) moved in a circle—or orbit—around Earth. It was in the nature of an ether-based object to behave this way.

Violent motion, on the other hand, describes movement that is contrary to an object's nature. Any movement that requires external force would be described as a violent motion. If, for example, you were to skip a stone along a river, the stone would require *your* force in order to move it through

Aristotle's version of a geocentric universe portrayed the stars and outer space as fixed.

the air and along the water. Since a stone would naturally move through the environment this way, this motion is described by Aristotle as violent motion. Most actions we observe or take in our day-to-day lives would be described as violent motion.

Gravity, Orbiting Objects, and Planetary Motion

Aristotle used these theories to "prove" that Earth was the center of the universe. In observation, it was easy to see that all objects—especially heavy ones—fell to the ground. The ground prevented them from moving closer to the center of the Earth. To Aristotle's eye, this meant that all heavy bodies strive to reach the center of Earth. To Aristotle, objects were striving for this center due to their own natural characteristics. In his mind, the logical result would be that Earth is the most central of all other bodies. He further justified this point by suggesting that the sky and the bodies found in it were lighter—made up of ether—and therefore rotating around the most central point, the center of the world.

In the two thousand years that Aristotelian physics ruled the world, Christianity came into being and spread through many developing nations. It would take many more discoveries and technological developments for scientists to begin to understand the missteps of Aristotle's logic and disprove it. And, unlike ancient Greece, these thinkers would have to face the Catholic Church. Where the beginning of civilizations saw mystic and scientific inquiry as being related, by the time of the Scientific Revolution, these two human endeavors would become a dividing factor, a fork in the road. And from the Scientific Revolution until now, these two modes of thinking have wandered further and further away from each other.

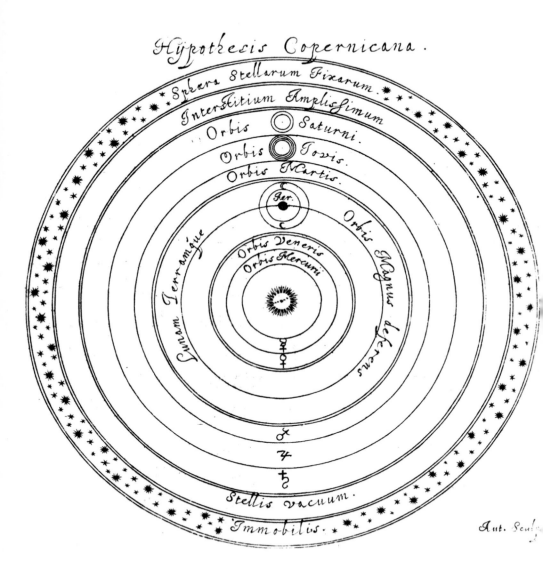

**Copernicus's heliocentric map wrongly
depicted planetary motion as perfectly circular.**

The Modern Understanding of Gravity and Planetary Motion

T he largest issue with Aristotelian physics was the lack
of information about gravity. The geocentric model of
the universe misunderstands the role of gravity in motion.
Though Aristotle did understand that all things fall to and
halt at the ground, the how and why of that phenomena was
rarely discussed or researched until the time of the Scientific
Revolution. At that time, Copernicus, Galileo, Kepler, and
Newton would oppose these long-held beliefs about physics.
Though the ideas came from physics, the rise of Christianity
meant that the world upheld geocentric beliefs through
religious impulse versus scientifically proven truth. These
thinkers faced enormous opposition and ultimately changed
history, utterly.

HELIOCENTRISM

The first big change in understanding the solar system as we know it today is moving from a geocentric image of the universe to a heliocentric one. After centuries of believing that Earth was the center of everything, it would take a lot of time and discovery to prove to the masses that, in fact, the sun was the center of our solar system.

This extreme shift in scientific thought occurred during the Scientific Revolution. During this time, modern science was born. From physics to astronomy to mathematics, chemistry, and biology, this intellectual movement changed views of nature drastically. The period began in Europe in 1543 when Nicolaus Copernicus dared to defy the Church and previous science, which stated that Earth was central to all existence. Copernicus's prediction that the sun was in fact the center of our solar system has been the basis for astronomy for centuries now.

The Copernican Revolution

Copernicus first wrote about his theory of **heliocentrism** in his 1543 book, *On the Revolutions of the Heavenly Spheres*. He started writing about his findings as early as 1514, but only released them to close friends or anonymously in fear that they went against the Church's scriptures about heaven and Earth.

Copernicus made tables of his astronomical observations. His detailed notes allowed him to predict past and future positions of stars and planets. While it seemed to the layperson that Earth stayed in place while the sky moved around it, by the time of Copernicus, it seemed that there were some oddities that geocentrism couldn't account for. Even today, if we keep an eye on certain star constellations and planets, they move in ways that can't be explained by a geocentric model of the solar system. Spotting planets in different locations in the sky, especially, shows that they appear to have moved *backwards* at different points in time. Until Copernicus suggested that perhaps Earth, too, was in orbit around something else—the sun—this phenomenon didn't fit the astronomical model of the time. Another reason this was hard to believe: scientists and the public believed if Earth were spinning on its axis, there would be insufferable amounts of wind.

Copernicus suggested that that planets revolve around a fixed sun and that the moon is the only body that revolves around Earth. Copernicus also noticed that other than the sun, planets made the same route through the sky *annually*. He deduced from that observation that Earth, too, must be following an orbit around the sun, since the sun was the only unmoving heavenly body. He observed that the sun gave light to all of the other heavenly bodies, further proving his theory that it was central.

To further his claims, Copernicus suggested that Earth was spinning on its axis each day, causing its twenty-four-hour cycle. Copernicus tried to stay in line with the geocentric model of the solar system by stating that the movements of heavenly bodies were, in fact, circular; the view from Earth would be the same whether it was fixed or moving because of these perfect circles.

According to Copernicus, stars were fixed, and the planets were in motion. To explain the seasons, the distance between Earth and the sun would have to change during orbits. If we look from Earth to the stars, we should see the stars from a different angle during the summer than we do doing the winter—this phenomenon is known as a **parallax.**

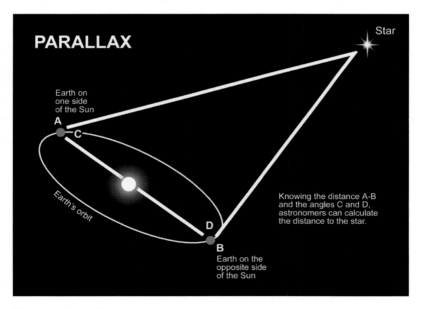

Diagram of a parallax

Gravity, Orbiting Objects, and Planetary Motion

This can be modeled in basic geometry with an isosceles triangle. If the bottom of the triangle represents Earth at opposite times of year, with the sun directly in the center of that line, then the furthest point of the triangle is a given star. The star should still be visible from either side based on this theory.

Unfortunately for Copernicus, a parallax was not observed. Copernican thinkers explained that the distance between Earth and the stars was so vast that parallax couldn't be observed between seasons. Copernicus wouldn't be proved right until 1838 when a parallax was first observed, nearly three hundred years after publishing *On the Revolutions of the Heavenly Spheres*.

Kepler's Laws

The next big advancement in astronomy came from Johannes Kepler. Kepler worked for Tycho Brahe, Copernicus's first major successor. When Brahe died, Kepler had access to all of Brahe's papers. Brahe had observed Mars and logged many other astronomical observations. These papers inspired Kepler and many others. Eventually, Kepler was able to advance Copernicus's theory of a heliocentric model with his own scientific ideas attached.

By studying Brahe's tables and making his own observations, Kepler noticed that solar and lunar eclipses possessed many strange qualities. For instance, shadow sizes during eclipses appeared disproportionate. During a lunar eclipse, the red color seen was seemingly unexplainable, and during a solar eclipse, the light surrounding the heavenly body was also seemingly unexplainable. He studied optics to try figuring out these astronomical mysteries.

In his book, *The Optical Part of Astronomy*, Kepler explored the relationship between light and sight. He modeled optics by using flat and curved mirrors, pinhole cameras, and astronomical geometry to show how eyes read light. He described the **inverse-square law**, which is still used in geometry and physics. This law says that an energy coming from a source spreads as it moves away. For example, light shining from a flashlight will be perceived with higher intensity over a smaller area of wall the closer the source is to the wall. As the light is brought farther away from the wall, the intensity will lessen, but the area of light will grow.

This understanding of light in relation to the human eye translated directly to light being cast onto spherical bodies. The basic description allowed Kepler to explain many phenomena, including a parallax. Another important discovery in his work on optics was the Principle of Continuity. Unlike a flash of light, the human eye can read light and focus on objects from different distances continuously. Kepler used parabolas and **ellipses** to model how the human eye can perceive things so quickly without losing focus.

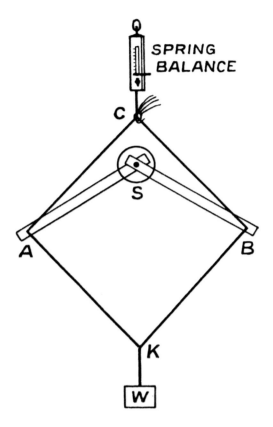

SPRING
BALANCE

Kepler's laws of motion rely on the physics behind a parallax and the inverse-square law.

As Kepler continued working, the sky presented something new to astronomers: a supernova of 1604, known now as Kepler's Supernova. A supernova is a star that explodes at the end of its life, causing a great brightness. When Kepler was alerted to the supernova, he became obsessed. He observed it and logged his findings for a year. With the help of Galileo, the two determined that there was no parallax in this instance. This proved that Aristotle was wrong about the heavens—they weren't fixed—and shook the Church's understanding of heaven entirely.

Kepler continued to publish many works that furthered Copernicus's theory of heliocentrism. He published three laws of planetary motion, Kepler's Laws of Planetary Motion, which are still studied today.

Galileo's Closer Looks

Notoriously, Kepler's works were largely ignored by Galileo Galilei—the most known and beloved figure of the Scientific Revolution. Galileo and Kepler were working at the same time to support Copernican theory, which caused an unspoken rivalry and distance between the two men and their work.

Galileo approached planetary motion from a slightly different view than Kepler. Where Kepler had the logs of his mentor to begin his mathematic endeavors, Galileo's contributions to understanding the solar system were based on his own observations.

In order to make qualitative observations about the heavens, Galileo needed to see better than those around him. He had heard a description of a telescope from an eyeglass maker in the Netherlands, Hans Lippershey. Yet Lippershey was unable to gain the patent for the telescope, and Galileo beat him to it. Galileo's telescope originally magnified things by 3x. Eventually, he'd refine his machine to magnify objects by 30x. We know the Galilean telescope today as a spyglass.

Galileo's first important finding with his spyglass were the moons of Jupiter. At first, he noted that three fixed stars were near Jupiter. As he observed Jupiter each day, he noticed that these stars changed positions. One night, one of these distant dots disappeared. When it reappeared a few days later, Galileo concluded that the dots were not fixed stars, but rather, bodies orbiting Jupiter. Eventually, he found a fourth body in orbit. He named these the Medician Stars to honor the Italian family in rule, the Medicis. However, the idea that smaller planets were orbiting another planet went against Aristotle's long-standing **cosmology**—cosmology that confirmed many creation claims in the Bible.

Despite the disbelief of the public, Galileo stuck to his scientific efforts. Through his spyglass, he observed many mysterious motions and objects in the night sky. Never before had humans been able to see stars or heavenly bodies closely and clearly. Galileo was the first to observe Saturn and see its rings. At the time, he didn't know what to make of these rings—were they planets? The mystery would outlive him.

Another important observation Galileo made through his spyglass also disproved the geocentric model of the universe: the planet Venus. In observing Venus, he noticed it appeared to have phases similar to the moon. This was proof of Copernicus's prediction that the universe was heliocentric, which stated that planets whose orbit was closer to the sun than Earth's would appear to us in phases. The explanation for this appearance lies in basic geometry and laws of light: since Venus is between Earth and the sun, the planet's terminator can be seen from Earth—what astronomers now call a stellar parallax.

Galileo was a pioneer, first to see and describe the surface of planets, the light of stars, and the nebulous mystery of a galaxy. He was also one of the first modern thinkers to clearly state that the laws of nature are mathematical. To that end, he came up with some mathematic theories along with his qualitative observations. Eventually, this would be an important step in science's separation from philosophy and religion. Science, for Galileo, required observations, experiments, and standards so that experiments and results could be replicated in different places to prove empirically true.

Aside from his observations that proved heliocentrism to be true, Galileo was the first to contribute to the next big change in the science of planetary motion: gravity. Though it wouldn't be known as gravity for some time to come, Galileo's laws of planetary motion were the seed for naming the phenomenon. As the story goes, a nineteen-year-old Galileo observed a priest swinging an altar lamp. No matter the length of the lamp's swing, the time it took to move back and forth seemed the same. This led to the invention of the pendulum clock.

More importantly, perhaps, it helped Galileo think about physics—acceleration, especially. Galileo hypothesized that Aristotle was wrong about the acceleration of objects when he claimed that heavier objects would fall faster than lighter ones. As the legend goes, Galileo dropped objects of different weights from the Leaning Tower of Pisa to prove that all objects fall at the same rate. But how would Galileo be able to measure the time each object took to fall? Ultimately, Galileo constructed simulations that led him to understand motion better than anyone of his time. Not only did Galileo predict the nature of objects in motion, but he began to question how and why objects suddenly stopped. Galileo was even able to name inertia, though it wouldn't be until later that the larger phenomena behind these motions would be named gravity.

GRAVITATION

As more and more evidence came to disprove Aristotelian cosmography, the public would have to accept and adapt to new knowledge of the universe. By the end of the seventeenth century, heliocentrism was generally accepted by the astronomy community. Eventually, the separation of religion and science veered further and further from each other, allowing both to begin to coexist.

From Copernicus to Kepler and Galileo, many qualitative and mathematic theories arose about the solar system. Missing from all three was the largest ruler of all: gravity. Gravity, even more so than planet orbits, is very difficult to imagine. No mechanical invention can make it visible to the naked eye. People have come to understand gravity as a ruling force because of the resulting behaviors of objects we can see.

Newton's Laws of Motion

Isaac Newton, an English physicist, began his work where Galileo left off: inertia. Nearly forty years after Galileo's death, Newton would write and publish *Mathematical Principles of Natural Philosophy*, a manifesto introducing formulas regarding the laws of motion and the introduction of **universal gravitation** to scientists and then the masses. Newton's views of motion and gravity would prevail for three more centuries, just as Aristotle's once had.

One key difference between Newton's work and the prior thinkers of the Scientific Revolution is the difference between description and explanation. Where the other thinkers were able to describe their theories and principles through a variety of expressions—from graphs to cosmography, to diagrams and numbers—Newton was able to explain these phenomena empirically.

Newton's work lays out, clearly, three laws of motion:

1. Every object in a state of uniform motion tends to stay in that state of motion unless an external force is applied to it. This is the law of inertia.
2. Acceleration occurs when a force acts upon a mass (object). The greater the mass, the greater the amount of force will be needed to accelerate the mass. This is expressed as $F=ma$ (force equals mass times acceleration).
3. For every action, there is an equal and opposite reaction.

Newton's Universal Gravitation

Following the logic of Newton's third law—that for every action, there is an equal and opposite reaction—Newton realized that a greater phenomenon was at play, especially when thinking about masses as big as planets. In Kepler's third law, the Law of Harmonies, Kepler assumes that the sun is stationary. But, if Newton's third law was true, he'd need to modify Kepler's understanding of how the planet's orbits relate to each other and the sun.

Further, as the legend goes, Newton's thoughts about motion came from seeing an apple fall from a tree. Since the apple was originally "at rest," hanging from a branch, Newton wondered what made it fall—what *force* acted upon it to make it *accelerate*? Newton figured there was a force he couldn't see acting upon the apple, which he called *gravity*. Newton also realized that the height of the apple did not impact the force acting upon it. Gravity could reach any apple at any height on any tree and cause the same acceleration of the apple toward the ground.

As Newton expanded his thoughts outward, he realized that the force was drawing the apple toward the center of Earth. If he imagined the whole of Earth and its spherical shape, the line between the apple's point of origin and where it landed on the ground would also be impacted by the Earth's spin. He expanded this into the idea of a cannon. If a cannon shot a projectile, it would eventually fall to Earth. If the magnitude of the shot changed, the projectile would have the same path proportional to its new force, always resulting in the projectile falling back to Earth.

From these thoughts, Newton came up with the Law of Universal Gravitation:

> *Every object in the universe attracts every other object with a force directed along the line of centers for the two objects that is proportional to the product of their masses and inversely proportional to the square of the separation between the two objects.*

Newton was able to prove his theory during his lifetime. He used his math to predict Neptune's existence.

Astronomers observed Uranus for nearly a year, noticing that its orbit was irregular. The irregularities were not explained by Newton's theories; however, Newton's law of universal gravitation suggested that the irregularities could be explained if the gravitational attraction of a yet-unknown planet were disturbing Uranus's motion. Scientists worked to create mathematical tables that would cause Uranus's journey in conjunction with another planet. Sure enough, the predictions led to the sighting of ever-distant Neptune. Newton's ideas reigned supreme for hundreds of years, changing physics and astronomy forever.

EINSTEIN'S RELATIVITY

Nearly three hundred years after Newton and the close of the Scientific Revolution, science prodigy Albert Einstein would enter the world with new theories about the nature of motion in our universe and beyond.

One main flaw in Newton's theory of universal gravitation was its inability to explain Mercury's volatile orbit. No scientist was able to find a body closer to the sun than Mercury to describe its behavior, as in Neptune to Uranus.

By 1915, Einstein had presented the world with his theories of special and general relativity. His laws would disprove many of Newton's claims, account for Mercury's strange orbital habits, and forever change physics, astronomy,

Time Dilation

Einstein imagined and described two observers in different spaceships moving through outer space to explain his conception of time. In one spaceship, an astronaut flashed a laser into a mirror. The laser beam came directly back down into a detector. This astronaut could barely tell he was moving at half the speed of light.

However, when an observer in a different spaceship was added to the scene, things got stranger. The observer would see the light move at a diagonal to hit the mirror, then down on another diagonal to hit the detector. Two different paths of light would be observed. The length of those paths wouldn't be the same. The time it takes for the laser to travel to the mirror is different for the first astronaut than it is for the observer. And this experience of time and space is relative to the speed of the object. This phenomenon is time dilation.

Time dilation becomes more and more crucial as things travel close to the speed of light. It's hard to understand on Earth, but when observing subatomic particles or huge objects in space, it becomes clear why this more precise understanding of motion has changed our perception of the universe and of time itself.

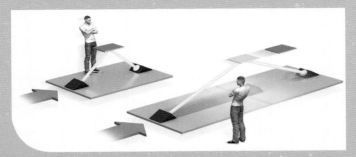

This diagram of time dilation shows two people's differing observations of a laser hitting a mirror and a detector.

cosmology, and the way people see the universe and its many mysterious objects.

Einstein realized that no object is ever really at rest. It's very hard to perceive this as humans because Earth is so much larger than we are, so we don't feel its constant motion. But even if we are seated on the ground, Earth is moving, and thus, we are moving too. Einstein wanted to account for this strange truth. In order to figure out the relationship between objects in motion more accurately than Newton did, Einstein explained that the frame of reference for each object needed to be accounted for.

In special relativity, he explained the math behind the motion of separate inertial frames of reference. The image Einstein used to describe this phenomenon was to describe a man sitting on a train and a man standing below the tracks. If the man on the train was sitting, he himself was at rest. But the moving train was his "reference-body." The man on the ground was also at rest, and his reference-body was the spinning Earth. The men were moving at constant speeds. Einstein would describe the perception of speed by each man in this situation as *relative* to the other, or how fast each man was moving was with respect to the other.

Special relativity needed to link space and time in a new way. Especially when bringing the ideas into outer space, where observers could free-fall in a spaceship, the observations of each other in motion needed a whole new plane to be understood—linked through Einstein's new constant, which was the speed of light.

It's very hard to imagine, but Einstein proposed four dimensions of space. The first three are typical: up and down, left and right, forward and backward. But then this issue of time became clear to him. Time had to occupy space. One easy way to know that this **space-time** continuum is real is the think of the unit light-years. Though it's measured in time, the measurement is of distance. It's why people see stars in the sky long after they've died—because it takes that long to see them from our distance.

$E = mc^2$

Though most of us don't know exactly what it means, many of us recognize Einstein's famous equation: $E = mc^2$. This equation explains the relationship between E (energy) and m (mass); c is the constant for the speed of light. The equation states that the closer an object gets to the speed of light, *the greater its mass becomes.* Therefore, the object goes faster, but it becomes heavier. Einstein was the first scientist to realize that energy and mass weren't separate, but instead, related. The heavier an object is, the more difficult it is to accelerate it. Though we can't actually move at c (at least not yet), if we could, our mass and energy would both be infinite. Energy can be turned into matter, and matter into energy. This revelation is known as conservation of mass-energy.

The Theory of General Relativity

Ten years after he presented the world with special relativity, Einstein presented general relativity. In his continued studies of space-time, Einstein was able to take physics further than Newton. Where Newton finally named the origin of falling bodies as gravity, Einstein was able to explain the origin of gravity itself.

General relativity encompassed more complicated reference-bodies. Where special relativity still took into account motions along a flat plane as we would draw in geometry, Einstein wanted to account for more complicated motions. If we take that plane—an x-y axis with coordinates—and curve it, what would happen?

Einstein described this as space-time. He said that the continuum is like the fabric of a trampoline. If a huge mass interacts with it, space-time becomes curved. Imagine placing a bowling ball at the center of a trampoline. What would happen? It would sink. If you subsequently placed smaller balls on the trampoline, what would they do? They would all fall toward the bowling ball. Unlike Newton's claim that things are mutually attracted to each other, Einstein proved that heavy objects warp the space-time continuum, causing us to experience and feel gravity.

Einstein wouldn't have to wait long to prove his theory right. In 1919, English astronomer Arthur Eddington

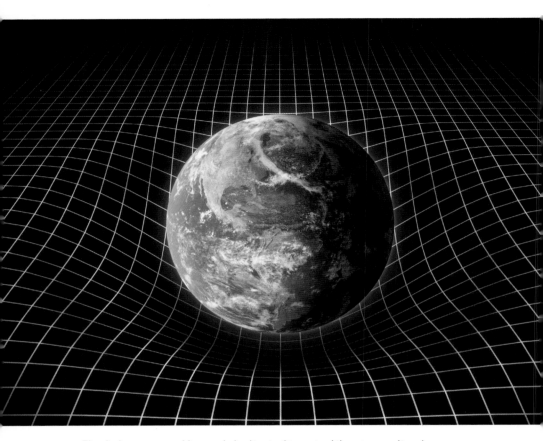

The dark area around heavenly bodies isn't empty. Like a trampoline, large bodies like planets warp the fabric of space-time.

travelled off the coast of West Africa to photograph a total eclipse. Einstein and Eddington predicted that a total solar eclipse would prove that Newton's science was off and that Einstein's new theories about physics were correct. Based on Einstein's work, light moving through space-time would also be affected by curvature, unlike Newton who did not believe that space was curved. As predicted by Einstein, when photos

Gravity, Orbiting Objects, and Planetary Motion

Eddington took before the eclipse and during the eclipse were compared, it appeared that the position of stars shifted when the sun was near.

Einstein predicted that Mercury's orbit precessed, or spun in a certain way, around the sun—it was elliptical in orbit, but more of an elliptical spiral than anything else. Just like the bowling ball on the trampoline, Mercury was attracted to where the sun had just been. Mercury's **precession** proved that space *and* time were warped by large masses, unlike Newton's theories of the past three hundred years.

Nicolaus Copernicus was the first to show that Earth revolved around the sun, making him the father of modern astronomy.

Scientists, Mathematicians, and Engineers

T he first significant contributions to our understanding
of modern science occurred during Europe's Scientific
Revolution. Today, we consider the revolution to have
begun in 1543 with the publication of Copernicus's *On
the Revolutions of the Heavenly Spheres.* The revolution was
considered complete when Newton published his *Principia*
in 1687. During these years, many new ways of thinking and
new inventions were used to unveil new truths about nature.

The three main figures of astronomy from this time were
Copernicus, Galileo, and Newton. They are each crucial to
our historic understanding of science. And they shared an
important characteristic: bravery. The Scientific Revolution
occurred at a time when the Church began to feel threatened
by the sciences. While the sciences were following Francis
Bacon's new philosophies about empiricism, or using
inductive methods for scientific inquiry, the invention of the

printing press was making the Bible available to the masses outside of Church. Bible studies could be conducted in one's home, without the prevailing interpretations of the Church. Because of this trying time for both science and the Catholic Church, the discoveries of these thinkers often put them in danger.

NICOLAUS COPERNICUS

Nicolaus Copernicus was a mathematician and astronomer from Royal Prussia (now Poland). He lived from 1473 to 1543. Copernicus was a deeply religious man. He studied papal law and worked as a Church physician and scholar in Poland after spending time in Italy. During his education, he became increasingly interested in the cosmos.

Though he was deeply religious, his understanding of the scientific method led him to new discoveries in the sky. In his observations, it became obvious to Copernicus that Earth was not the center of the universe. Copernicus theorized a heliocentric model of the solar system by 1514.

Because his findings went against the creation myth of the Bible, Copernicus wasn't sure how to present his radical findings to the world without facing backlash. Furthermore, during that time, findings were presented to leaders of the Church before they were disseminated to the public. Yet Copernicus wrote his theories as the printing press became popular for public transmission of texts.

Copernicus gave his work only to friends at first. He also printed his ideas anonymously. For thirty years, his ideas about heliocentrism were hidden from public view. Many astronomers believed Copernicus's findings. They even presented his ideas in lectures that were attended by Church leaders. But, as predicted, the Church did not approve of Copernican theory. In 1539, before Copernicus's book was published, Martin Luther reminded scientists and the public that the Bible didn't approve of these thoughts, quoting that "Joshua commanded the sun to stand still and not the earth."

Copernicus had a stroke at the age of seventy. Legend has it that a completed version of his book, *On the Revolutions of the Heavenly Spheres*, was placed in his hands on his deathbed. He awoke from his coma to see his life's work fulfilled and then died peacefully. Scientists would use his findings as the basis for a new model of the solar system for years to come.

GALILEO GALILEI

One of human history's greatest figures, Galileo was born in 1564 in Pisa, Italy. Known still as the "Father of Modern Science," Galileo was a force to be reckoned with—by other scientists and more notably, the Catholic Church.

When Galileo was nineteen, he observed a priest swinging an altar lamp. The symmetry of the swinging led him to reconsider many phenomena of physics. One of our

When Galileo's body was being reburied one hundred years after his death, a fanatic snipped off part of his middle finger, now on display in a museum.

many mythic images of Galileo is the young man in the Leaning Tower of Pisa dropping objects of various weights to the ground in his falling-body experiments. Though we can't be sure if this really happened, the image helps us understand one of Galileo's great contributions to mechanical physics: that an object's mass does not impact its acceleration through space. This idea also led him to many important inventions we still use today, such as the pendulum clock. His most notable invention was the first telescope.

Galileo and his telescope quickly became the emblem of the Scientific Revolution. Galileo was the first to see and document many features of planets, the moon, and constellations up close. Imagine a time before there were photographs. Other than what we can see with the naked eye, images of these heavenly bodies were scarce. To make matters more complicated, what Galileo found supported Copernicus's theory that the universe was heliocentric, not geocentric.

During his time, Galileo was as well known for his arrogance as he was for his genius. Not only was he disinterested in the publications of his contemporaries, but he was loud about it. Likewise, he loudly spoke out against the Church. Despite being deeply religious, Galileo saw empirical evidence in the motion of heavenly bodies that physically proved Aristotle and the creation myths of the Church were incorrect. In 1616, Pope Paul V of the Catholic Church publicly denounced Galileo's findings and banned him from speaking or teaching in the defense of Copernican thinking again.

Galileo refused to abide by the Church's request. He published a work called *Dialogue Concerning the Two Chief World Systems* in 1632. Galileo argued the piece was neutral, but in it, three men discuss heliocentric ideals of the universe. One man is for Copernican thinking, one is against it, and one is impartial. In the text, the man who supports

Aristotle's ideas about geocentrism comes off as being more simpleminded than the others.

The Catholic Church promptly summoned Galileo to Rome for a trial. After threats of torture, Galileo finally confessed to having supported Copernican thinking despite being banned from such philosophies. He was charged with heresy, or holding an opinion that disagrees with the official position of the Church. For his crime, Galileo was sentenced to house arrest for the rest of his life. For the next nine years, he continued to study and write until he suffered heart failure in 1642. It took the Church over 100 years to lift the ban on Copernican theory. Nearly two hundred years after Galileo's death, in 1835, the Church finally dropped its public opposition to heliocentrism.

In 1992, Pope John Paul II officially apologized on the Catholic Church's behalf for how Galileo was treated. Today, we still use telescopes to make new discoveries about space, and we still use his methods of observation and inquiry (and his math) to understand mechanical physics. Not only was he central to the story of the Scientific Revolution, but he remains the "Father of Modern Science" today.

ISAAC NEWTON

For many, the Scientific Revolution ends with Galileo's second-to-last publication, *Dialogue Concerning the Two Chief World Systems*. However, others view Isaac Newton's

Along with his many accomplishments regarding gravity, Newton also advanced the study of optics and is the father of calculus in mathematics.

publication of *Mathematical Principles of Natural Philosophy* (often referred to as *Principia*) as the proper finale. Known as the revolution's "grand synthesis," *Principia* used empiricism to elaborate upon Copernican theory and Galileo's discoveries, and expand the heliocentric model to include a new phenomenon: gravity. Nowadays, we can't imagine walking through the world without knowing of gravity.

Isaac Newton was born in 1643, exactly one year after Galileo's death. When Newton was about forty years old, he published *Principia*, which described his laws of motion and named and explained universal gravitation. It is still considered the most influential book ever written on physics, if not the most influential on science at large.

Like many great thinkers, a myth follows the legacy of Newton's work. In our telling and retelling of his story, as a young boy, he sat beneath an apple tree and discovered the mysteries of the universe. As the story goes, Newton had his "Eureka!" moment when an apple fell from a tree and hit him on the head. Though it's been disproved that this happened in reality, there is an account in which Newton considers apple trees and describes an important question: why does an apple *always* fall perpendicular to the ground? The idea that something is *always* true is an important root in the tree of science. When naming a principle or a theory, a scientist must figure that the rules of physics are always true, otherwise, they've not been stated correctly yet.

Newton was instantly famous upon publishing his work. Like Galileo, he was not very cooperative with others. His ideas were his own, and while this gave him an air of genius, it also led to paranoia and isolation. He had many conflicts with others, especially his long-standing nemesis from his college years, Robert Hooke. Hooke accused Newton of plagiarism. Newton took Hooke out of all of his notes. Newton wouldn't become the president of England's Royal Society until Hooke's death in 1705. While president, he was a tyrant. He made more enemies and lorded his fame and power over his contemporaries as well as new scientists.

Newton died in 1727, and his fame only grew after his death. Scientists and laypeople began to understand physics more clearly. Everything from sailing a boat to understanding tides became more common knowledge for all. It wouldn't be until the turn of the twentieth century that Einstein would disprove any of Newton's theories. Even today, Newton's work with mechanical physics is so close to accurate that we use it in our day-to-day lives. But as technology would advance drastically, physics would need to advance with it.

PLANETARY MOTION FROM THE TWENTIETH CENTURY UNTIL NOW

The key element that Newton's work did not account for was energy. Albert Einstein came along in the early 1900s to change everything we know about the universe. This may seem cliché, but not since Newton had anyone named— in math—deep truths about the way the universe works and *why*. Einstein has become synonymous with genius. Einstein's presentation of relativity helped humanity enter the twentieth century. From subatomic particles, to the prediction of black holes, to the atomic bomb, to landing on the moon, and GPS on our phones, everything we do— especially relating to technology—in our day-to-day lives is impacted by Einstein's thoughts.

Because of Einstein's great contributions to science, the world has changed. Many institutions have since been established to continue work in physics and astronomy especially. Just as observatories came into being after Galileo's invention of the telescope, institutions like NASA have been able to venture into deeper corners of space than ever before because of Einstein's ideas and the math to back them up.

Albert Einstein

Einstein was born in 1879 in Germany. He died in 1955 in America. His lifetime spanned a time of huge changes in human history—Einstein lived through both world wars. Einstein's theory of special relativity was presented in 1905 and general relativity was presented in 1915. World War I began at the end of 1914 when Austria's Archduke was assassinated. Einstein's relativity led to a Nobel Prize in 1921, just three years after WWI ended. A decade after his win, he was targeted by the Nazis and had to flee Germany.

Though Einstein was not a soldier, his German-Jewish heritage and the time of war are an interesting backdrop to his findings. Although he is still known for his humanitarian efforts, his work in relativity, advanced electromagnetic studies, and quantum physics led to the invention of the atomic bomb. Einstein, like many more scientists these days, represents the complicated relationship between scientists and warfare.

Despite his pacifism, Einstein advocated work on an atomic bomb in order to beat the Nazis to such a discovery.

Despite Einstein's amazing test scores, he had a hard time finding work after school. He ended up working as a clerk at a patent office in Switzerland by 1902. Einstein used this time to develop his theorems, which quickly became the principle of relativity. Unlike many scientists who follow the letter of the scientific method, Einstein's work was written as a **gedankenexperiment**, or thought-experiment. This combined the scientific method with his own imagination.

He used imagination to draw out a scenario and describe the motion of objects in vivid detail. Then he would use mathematic principles to label his imagined scene.

Einstein was able to consider the speed of light and energy in ways that his predecessors could not. Since the Scientific Revolution, many inventions presented new ways of seeing the world. Thanks to photography, X-rays, radium, uranium, and more, people were able to look more deeply into electromagnetism than ever before. These inventions and the discoveries they brought to the world allowed Einstein to rethink the world at its smallest and largest states—the atomic level and in outer space.

Einstein's special relativity was confusing to many. But a famous physicist, Max Planck, backed Einstein's assertions. Planck is known as the father of quantum mechanics. His endorsement allowed the young Einstein to continue working and publishing until his theories were proven true. And they continue to be proven true today.

Einstein's predictions about relativity were first proven true in 1919 during a total solar eclipse. In those days—before digital technology—the scientists had to figure out where they'd be able to observe an eclipse from, needing to consider global positioning and the clearest weather. Overnight, the discovery that, as Einstein predicted, light did in fact bend along space-time as it neared a gravitational origin made him famous.

Stephen Hawking

One of the many phenomena Einstein predicted was the existence of black holes. Black holes were not discovered in Einstein's lifetime. The famous physicist Stephen Hawking has been able to use Einstein's work to continue proving the merits of relativity in the context of planetary motion, planetary creation, and other phenomena in space.

Stephen Hawking was born in England in 1942. As a child, like many prodigies, Hawking did not perform well in school. Though he cared little for the rules of school, he was constantly playing and inventing board games, pondering the sky, and generally engaging in introverted, intellectual endeavors. Hawking's bright mind, despite his lack of studying, got him admission to Oxford by the age of seventeen.

Since Oxford didn't offer a degree in mathematics at the time, Hawking chose to study physics. He considered himself a cosmologist—a scientist who uses astronomy and physics to study the development of the universe. He went on to Cambridge to get a PhD in cosmology.

At the young age of twenty-one, while at Cambridge, Hawking was diagnosed with amyotrophic lateral sclerosis—better known today as ALS or Lou Gehrig's disease. The result of this disease is the inability to control or use your muscles. Hawking was given about two years to live. Though

Hawking is one of the most important living scientists; his ideas have changed how we see the universe.

his life is drastically different since his diagnosis, he is still alive today. (He uses a wheelchair, has twenty-four-hour care, and uses a special computer to be able to communicate and continue his work as a physicist.)

Early in his career, Hawking threw himself vigorously into his scientific inquiries about how the universe began. One of his colleagues, Roger Penrose, made exciting findings about the fate of stars and the creation of black holes. The two of them worked together to expand upon the idea of the big bang theory—the idea that because the universe is expanding, at some point further back in time and space, the universe emerged from a small state of condensed, hot matter. The idea of a single origin point for the universe is referred to as a singularity.

A singularity, according to Einstein's prediction and Hawking and Penrose's work, is not as simple as a starting point the way we might imagine it. Rather, it specifically relates to the way that space-time functions. If the fabric of space-time can bend infinitely, then a point with this infinite curvature would be a space-time singularity. If it were possible to follow space-time back (in distance and time) far enough to the big bang, you'd find the original singularity.

Einstein was first to predict the existence of black holes in his theory of general relativity. Hawking and Penrose were able to do the mathematic proofs required to prove that black holes exist as well as describe their properties. These contributions are especially significant to the world because black holes could not be observed—to be close to a black hole is certain death, for nothing can escape its gravitational tug, not even light. Until digitization, GPS, telescopes, and satellite advancement became more normalized, observation and mathematic experimenting were the prominent modes of solving these mysteries for much of the twentieth century.

Although many assumed that a black hole functioned like a vacuum, Hawking proved that black holes emit radiation. This radiation is known today as Hawking radiation. A key property of a black hole is an event horizon. This boundary in space-time only allows matter to pass inward. Nothing can escape the event horizon, including light. Think of it this way: an event along space-time indicates where and when a given event occurred (in all four dimensions). If light entering a black hole cannot exit, then it can't be observed. Therefore, there is no residual proof that the event occurred at all. It's a bit similar to that age-old philosophical question: if a tree falls in the woods, and no one is there to hear it, did it make a sound? The difference is that, unlike coming upon a fallen tree in the woods, there would be no evidence whatsoever that an event occurred. For example, if light from a sun travelled into a black hole, and subsequently, the sun of origin died, there would be no remnants left to prove that sun existed in the first place.

Hawking showed that black holes, in fact, emitted radiation, despite the appearance and behavior of an event horizon. By predicting radiation, Hawking then proved that the more mass a black hole takes in, the cooler it gets. Further, the inverse is true: when a black hole emits radiation, the energy comes from the black hole itself, and so, it loses mass. This is taken directly from Einstein's famous equation $E = mc^2$.

NASA

The ideas of these figures would be nothing without empirical proof that their theories are in fact laws that rule physics. To that end, since the Scientific Revolution, many inventions and institutions have been at the helm of discovery with regard to astronomy. The leading institution in space exploration is NASA.

NASA stands for the National Aeronautics and Space Administration. Run by the United States federal government, NASA runs space programs as well as research programs. NASA was started by President Dwight D. Eisenhower in 1958. Though we often think of the "space race" in conjunction with the Cold War, Eisenhower began NASA as a civilian program, not a branch of the military. The goal was to understand Earth better by observing it from a distance, to build spaceships, and to make observations and discoveries in space.

By 1961, though, the space race was underway when the Soviets sent an astronaut into space for four days. President John F. Kennedy set a goal to safely land on the moon by the end of the 1960s. In July of 1969, *Apollo 11* successfully landed on the moon. Neil Armstrong was the first man to step foot on the moon, followed by Buzz Aldrin. Though the image taught to us by history is of the American flag on the moon (and Neil Armstrong's voice saying "One small

The Smithsonian Air and Space Museum

One of America's premiere museums, the Smithsonian's Air and Space Museum, has many NASA artifacts on display. Located in the nation's capital, Washington, DC, the museum holds the largest collection of aircraft and spacecraft in the world. If we think all the way back to Aristotle, Galileo, Newton, and Einstein, it's fascinating to realize that their images of this planet and the heavenly bodies resulted in the artifacts in this museum.

The first airplane, the *Spirit of St. Louis*, might remind us of a bird flying as described by Newton's laws. In order for man to replicate the bird, he needed those ideas of Newton's. The spacecraft *Apollo 11* is an emblem of our first human encounter on a heavenly body—something Aristotle and Galileo could only have dreamed of, something that Einstein almost lived long enough to watch.

One exhibit at the museum is "Exploring the Planets." At the center of the exhibit is a full-scale replica of a Voyager. The Voyager robots were built to replicate human senses. The data collected by the Voyagers has deepened our understanding of our solar system's farthest planets. We now have photographs and understanding of Jupiter, Saturn, Uranus, and Neptune, each as vivid and different as our own special planet.

Other highlights of the exhibit include the Mars Exploration Rover and the Surveyor Television Camera. Though many of us will never fly to the moon or Mars, we can see the videos taken by these special robots and learn about the geology of other heavenly bodies.

step for man, one giant leap for mankind"), the mission has a legacy beyond a photo opportunity. In conjunction with the missions that followed, Apollo 11 brought a wealth of new information about the solar system to mankind. From observations, to soil samples, to measurements of **solar wind**, magnetic fields, and more, scientists in physics, astronomy, and cosmology now had new information and new means of understanding planets and planetary motion. None of those missions would have been possible without understanding gravity and relativity. Without those early thinkers, perhaps no one would have predicted that there'd be no gravity on the moon, even!

NASA's work continues to impact science in many ways. Not just in the fields named earlier, but also in technology, communications, and aviation. The research done at NASA to conduct these kinds of missions has advanced technology in many ways.

The works of these thinkers and the subsequent inventions, math equations, and feats of engineering that have come from their ideas have helped humans collect a wealth of knowledge about the universe. While there are still many unsolved mysteries, technologies invented since Einstein's theories have allowed humanity to dive deeper and deeper into space-time than ever before. And from these technologies, our models of the solar system and the larger universe have become increasingly clear.

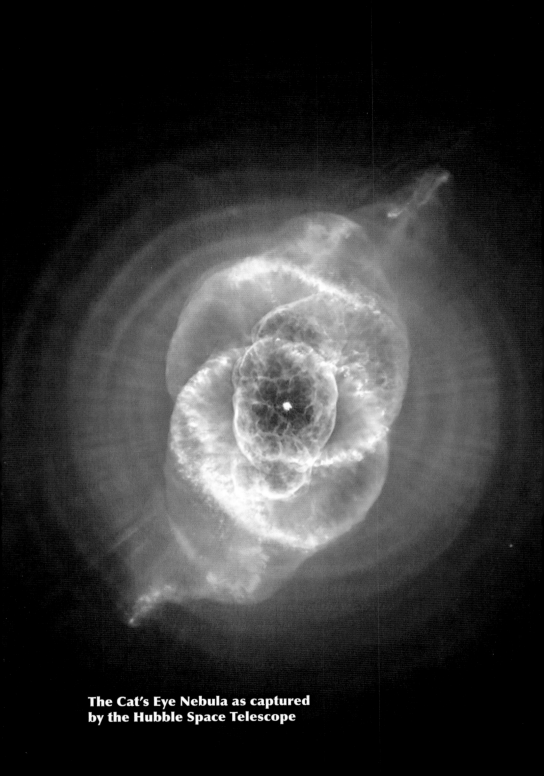

The Cat's Eye Nebula as captured by the Hubble Space Telescope

Visualizing Gravity

G ravity is a phenomenon that impacts our lives all day every day. Despite its powers, gravity is very hard to imagine because it's invisible. We only know it exists based on the motions and behaviors of objects. Though we can't see gravity, we notice it as the Earth spins constantly, as we are able to stay on the ground, as the moon moves around us, and as an apple falls from a tree as the myth of Newton's universal gravitation described so long ago. From Aristotle to now, though, scientists and advancing technologies have been able to visualize gravity on Earth, in our solar system, and in the universe beyond.

FROM ANCIENT TIMES THROUGH THE SCIENTIFIC REVOLUTION

Early models of Earth and other heavenly bodies were diagrammed, primarily, by hand. As we've seen in the earliest drawings of the Earth, scientists used everything from clay tablets to parchment, and eventually paper, to render visualized diagrams of what they imagined was happening in the sky.

Geometry

One of the basic ways measuring and diagramming nature came into being is through geometry. Geometry allows mathematicians and scientists to figure out the placement of planets and stars, as well as represent their relations to each other.

A common geometric phenomenon still used to measure distances between planetary bodies is a parallax. From the Greek, meaning "alteration," a parallax is the difference between the apparent position of an object viewed along two lines of sight. If you place your thumb in front of your face and close one eye, when you switch which eye is closed, it will *appear* that the finger has moved. The effect is a parallax.

Astronomers can use a parallax to measure the position of nearby stars. First, they make an account of the apparent distance of a given star and its relationship to the stars behind it. Then, six months later, they measure those same stars again. Because Earth is on the opposite side of its orbit, the shift—though small—can be measured. Earth's position in the first case is like the first open eye looking at the thumb, while its second position is like the second eye.

Since parallaxes of nearby stars are very small, the ancient Greeks couldn't use this process as efficiently as we can with the tools of today. Without telescopes, satellites, and other digital advances, the ancient Greeks mistakenly observed a lack of parallaxes. This led them to believe that Earth was not orbiting the sun.

VISUALIZING THE UNIVERSE IN THE TWENTIETH CENTURY

Einstein's theory of relativity changed everything about the human understanding of science across many realms— culture, military relations, philosophy, quantum physics, spirituality, and the great beyond that is the universe. Einstein's discoveries were made possible by early quantum physicists, studies in electromagnetism, the discovery of radium, and inventions that changed the way we could see things more closely.

Einstein's work began in gedankenexperiments—like his predecessors, he vividly used language to model his ideas. Paired with empirical math, Einstein's gedankenexperiments are the foundation of everything we know now about the

How Hubble Works

The Hubble Space Telescope makes one full orbit around Earth every ninety-seven minutes. That's about 5 miles (8 kilometers) per second. At that speed, you could cross the United States in ten minutes. Like any good telescope, Hubble's precision is based on carefully shaped and placed glass and mirrors. Hubble's main mirror captures light and sends it to another mirror. This second mirror bounces the light back at the first mirror and through a tiny hole at the center (like a pinhole camera). From there, the light is sent to Hubble's various science instruments.

The power of a telescope is not in its ability to magnify. Rather, it collects more light than the human eye can. This is also true of high-quality cameras and their lenses. Hubble has a few instruments to read light. Hubble hosts a few **spectrographs**, which read ultraviolet and infrared light. Things that were once invisible become visible because these machines can read more light than our own eyes can. Hubble also has a few complex cameras that capture survey information about different things in our universe, such as **dark energy** and dark matter. Because the conditions of space are so hostile, Hubble has sensors that help it take clear photographs. One is a heat sensor, which allows it to transfer heat from infrared light into a light reading. Objects that humans can't see because of our inability to see infrared light have since become visible—deep space and birth sites for stars are two things we've seen through obstacles such as **interstellar dust**.

universe. While many aspects of relativity were proven during Einstein's lifetime, advancements made by engineers and scientists in visualizing the universe through digital technologies have let us see many of Einstein's predictions, thus proving them. From the twentieth century and into the twenty-first, digitization has allowed us to see planetary motion in a whole new way.

Photography and Telescopes

Telescopes, photographs, and motion photography have helped us visualize and record all kinds of phenomena in the universe. Along with optics, advancements in digitization have allowed our visualization—be it documentary style or animated—to be far more precise than early astronomers could have dreamed possible.

Perhaps our most famous characterization of these advancements is the Hubble Space Telescope. In 1990, NASA launched the Hubble Space Telescope into the universe. Though the first space telescope—the Stargazer—was launched in 1968, the Hubble is our most well known for its size and abilities. Despite advanced technologies and top-of-the-line observatories, a ground telescope cannot compare to one that is orbiting in space.

Hubble orbits Earth above the atmosphere. Therefore, it can see without distorted or blocked light. Though many other space telescopes have come along since, Hubble is the

The improvements to Hubble's spectrograph resulted in advancements in breast cancer treatment, as NASA's silicon chips are now used for tissue imaging.

Gravity, Orbiting Objects, and Planetary Motion

only one designed to be serviced by space astronauts. Instead of bringing Hubble down to Earth, astronauts go up and make sure everything is running correctly. Crews have fixed mirrors, made additions to the telescope, and completed other maintenance.

Many of us have encountered images taken by Hubble in newspapers and classrooms. Hubble is especially important because it can be accessed by the public. Hubble's mission is about learning for all, and access to knowledge for all; anyone can apply for time on the telescope. Without the background light experienced on Earth, the images taken are of extraordinarily high resolution. This imaging has helped us clarify our vision of the universe.

From Saturn's rings, to **extrasolar planets**, to **gamma ray bursts**, Hubble has shown the world parts of the universe that could not have been predicted based on observation with the naked eye of ancient Greece, Galileo's telescope, or even the finest observatory. Hubble's evidence in photographs has also presented us with more proof of space-time. Fragments of the **early universe** can be captured by Hubble. Because light travels in light-years, many of Hubble's images are of things that occurred in the past. Unlike digging up a fossil, these images from the past haven't yet reached us. One big discovery of Hubble's was of toddler galaxies— galaxies from the time the universe was still young. Hubble has showed us protoplanetary disks, which are made of dense gas and dust and surround new stars. Detecting the early universe of billions of years ago has helped us develop more precise math to prove the laws of physics.

Hubble's discoveries have changed our vision of the universe entirely. Images from Hubble have proven many new insights about the universe to be true. One of Hubble's main discoveries is the relative age of the universe—somewhere between thirteen and fourteen billion years. Hubble also discovered dark energy, showing scientists that the universe is expanding.

Hubble's parts are degrading over time; the telescope won't be operational forever. When Hubble ceases operation, its orbit around Earth will degrade and it will spiral back toward us, just as other **space junk** eventually does. Because of the way Hubble was designed, it will eventually de-orbit with the help of a robot and fall into an ocean.

Satellites

The idea of an artificial satellite has been around since at least the time of Newton. He published mathematical descriptions of the possibility of satellites being used to help astronomers. Satellites also began appearing in early science fiction works during the 1800s.

Satellites came to the forefront as a possibility during the late 1920s. With the invention and rise of radio technologies, telephones, and the like, satellites offered a technological

Sputnik I

possibility. Austro-Hungarian rocket engineer Herman Potocnik was the first to imagine and detail a space station, an orbiting spacecraft that could be used to observe Earth and other planetary bodies and send information to the ground through radio technology. Other scientists and fiction writers would take this idea further and consider possibilities for mass communications.

In 1957, the Soviet Union launched the world's first satellite, *Sputnik 1*, into space to orbit Earth. This began the space race between the United States and the Soviet Union, or the USSR. *Sputnik 1* ran on batteries and delivered a radio bleep to announce itself. For the first time, people could look at the night sky and see a manmade object cruise by. *Sputnik 1* gave scientists information as well. The main information delivered was to identify the density of high atmospheric layers based on its orbit. Shortly after *Sputnik 1*, which lasted for twenty-two days on its battery, *Sputnik 2* was sent into orbit with a living passenger—a dog named Laika.

The largest satellite orbiting Earth is the International Space Station (ISS). The ISS was first launched in 1998 and is still in orbit today. It has what is called a low Earth orbit and can be seen with the naked eye. One huge advancement in visualizing and understanding gravity has been the experience of the lack of it. The ISS is a zero-gravity laboratory. It's been inhabited continuously by astronauts for over fifteen years. On the ISS, astronauts

The International Space Station is the most expensive object ever built, costing about $100 billion.

conduct experiments in all kinds of scientific fields—physics, astronomy, meteorology, biology, and more. Scientists on the ground have access to the data gathered on the space station. Besides observing Earth from a distance, research found on the space station also relates to understanding space weather.

In questioning the universe, scientists wanted to be able to know and see more of it. From dark matter to black holes to dying stars, astronauts and scientists wanted to use the ISS to understand more than just weather. Engineers and scientists worked together to invent the Alpha Magnetic Spectrometer (AMS). The AMS is a machine that detects particles. It was conceived and invented at one of the world's leading universities, the Massachusetts Institute of Technology (MIT). Because space is hostile to life (as we humans experience it), understanding the smallest bits of space is as important as the larger phenomena. This ideal recalls the work of Einstein. Einstein's belief that the laws of physics will be true in every circumstance allowed him to understand physics at the quantum level as well as the larger universe.

One prediction of Einstein's about space (later proven by Stephen Hawking), is that energy ruled all. From light to radiation, the large masses of objects in space (as well as the condensed, atomic version as in the big bang), result in a high radiation field—one unsuitable for human life. The ISS, with the help of the AMS, has been able to read, understand, and offer visual representation of that radiation field. From the subatomic particles left by solar wind and **cosmic rays**, the AMS has given us evidence of high vacuum, high radiation, **microgravity**, and extreme temperatures.

Space Travel

Besides human activity on satellites like the ISS, space travel is something that's enamored humans for centuries.

Neil Armstrong took this photo of Buzz Aldrin walking on the surface of the moon.

After the launch of *Sputnik*, the United States launched its own satellite, the *Explorer*. The real competition that these satellites were the precursor to, though, was human travel and experience in outer space. In this race, the United States won, becoming the first country to put a man on the moon.

The satellite information from *Sputnik* and *Explorer* was able to help astronauts predict and prepare for space travel.

Apollo 2 was an unmanned space mission. Though it orbited Earth four times, it was destroyed six hours after takeoff.

From zero-gravity, to anticipating the drastic atmospheric differences, and knowing precisely the time it would take to travel to and from the moon, a lot of research and knowledge about gravity was gathered before NASA's *Apollo 11* would deliver Neil Armstrong and Buzz Aldrin to step foot on the moon.

Between *Sputnik* and *Apollo 11*, other rocket and satellite missions went into space to collect data and prepare the astronauts. During many of those journeys, issues of engineering and technology arose—both for the United States and the USSR. *Apollo 1*, for example, caught fire during a ground test and killed its crew. NASA learned about construction flaws that prevented the crew from escaping the fire. The USSR's *Soyuz* rocket also suffered from design flaws, leading to the first in-flight fatality. Once both teams slowed down and reconfigured their expectations about the conditions of outer space—especially with regard to incoming information about atmospheric pressure, microgravity, and the like, NASA was eventually able to successfully fulfill a moon landing. It took almost ten years, a lot of funding, and a tremendous amount of technological advancement to build machines that could exit the atmosphere and Earth's gravitational pull to make it to the moon and back, let alone to figure out how two men could walk on the moon and make it back alive.

As our interactions with technologies become more and more natural, the questions we raise about the past and future have broader possibilities. Hubble's images teach us about many phenomena in the universe. They also help us ponder what else is out there. New ideas may seem like science fiction to us now, but as we know from recent history, science fiction eventually can become reality.

The Doppler Effect and Einstein's relativity are crucial ideas behind how and why GPS works.

5

Orbiting Objects and Planetary Motion Today and Tomorrow

O ur new abilities to visualize the universe—as it was billions of years ago, now, and in the future—have changed the human relationship to space. Though most of us will never know as much as a physicist or astronomer about the many mysterious objects of outer space, our own interaction with it grows through technology every single day.

SOME EVERYDAY ORBITING OBJECTS

When we think of Earth from space, most of us think of pristine images of a perfect sphere against a black backdrop— our perfect, mythic marble. Nowadays, though, Earth is surrounded by hundreds of thousands of orbiting objects.

It's easy to go online and see live and CGI models of objects orbiting Earth right this second.

Most of the things in low Earth orbit, or LEO, are satellites. From our phones to TV, to weather, the military, and beyond, we are constantly using satellites to know the time, weather, and our position in the world. Technology has made it easy to track and see these objects and the paths they take every day.

GPS

One object we use more and more every day is the Global Positioning System (GPS). Whether we are looking at our phones to find a new coffee shop, taking a long road trip, or checking out Google Maps, an orbiting object is keeping track of us and keeping us on track. GPS is possible because of Einstein's theory of relativity. Though he wasn't alive to benefit from this invention, we all have him to thank; without him, we'd be lost.

GPS was originally built for military navigation and initially cost over $10 billion. Twenty-four satellites orbit Earth carrying a precise atomic clock in order to give us a GPS standard in real time. Each satellite moves very quickly, enough to orbit Earth twice per day. Einstein's theory of special relativity states that the more rapidly a clock moves, the slower it ticks. The change in speed is practically unnoticeable to us; however, over time, these millionths of a second add up. Another complexity of GPS relates to general relativity. Gravity for the satellites is four times weaker than gravity on the ground. Because Einstein's general theory predicts (rightly) that gravity curves space-time, orbiting clocks will tick slightly faster. Basically, a GPS satellite clock ticks faster than a clock on the ground.

The atomic clock on the satellite, therefore, must be very precise in order to account for the time lapse between emitted signal and delivered signal. The GPS electronically adjusts the rates of the satellite clocks each day to make up the difference in measurement relative to time that passes on the ground.

Not only is GPS a feat of understanding orbits, but it returns our understanding to us. GPS is used for far more than finding your closest Starbucks. It can be used for airplane navigation, sailing, oil exploration, and military endeavors. GPS devices can determine location within an instant. Though many of these systems can be very expensive; nowadays, GPS is commonplace, right on your smartphone. Even if you lose your phone, it will keep track of itself.

Space Junk

With many manmade objects going into space, there has already been a lot of **orbital debris**, or manmade objects orbiting Earth that no longer function. This space junk includes everything from abandoned satellites to broken pieces of satellites and space telescopes, parts of rockets, random objects, and even human waste.

More than 500,000 pieces of space junk that can be tracked are orbiting Earth. The oldest known piece of orbital debris is a satellite from 1964. The *Vanguard 1*, which launched in 1958, stopped working in 1964. Before man walked on the moon, man simply "walked" in space by exiting the craft during a mission. Astronaut Ed White famously lost his glove in 1965 on a space walk. More recently, an ammonia reservoir (part of the ISS) the size of a refrigerator became orbital debris.

This moving landfill is very dangerous. NASA's chief scientist for orbital debris, Nicholas Johnson, says that "the greatest risk to space missions comes from nontrackable debris." Like active satellites, this orbital debris whizzes around Earth at high speeds. Orbits of debris differ in direction, plane, and speed, making collisions very plausible. Miraculously not that many disasters have happened yet. But a few have.

In 1996, fragments from an exploded French rocket damaged a French satellite in a collision. In 2007, China used a missile to destroy an old weather satellite. This action produced at least 3,000 pieces of space junk. In 2009, a Russian satellite destroyed an active US satellite in a collision, resulting in over 2,000 pieces of trackable debris. While we have many trackable pieces of debris because of GPS, imaging, and other technologies, there are many pieces of space junk that aren't accounted for. In either case, the threat of harm to space missions is high. The speeds of these defunct objects as well as their changed orbital patterns suggest that even something as small as a fleck of paint could present a hazard.

NASA and the Department of Defense take tracking orbital debris very seriously. They have extensive catalogues of objects in Earth's orbit. They've also worked together to categorize objects and their subsequent debris. Thus far, at least twenty thousand pieces of debris orbiting Earth are larger than a softball. About five hundred thousand pieces of debris are at least marble-sized. NASA and the Department of Defense categorize collision risks based on object size. Small enough particles can, for example, be avoided by using debris shields. These shields, though, are not strong enough to withstand collision with larger objects.

Space junk has caused NASA to learn new things about orbiting objects. The institution has conducted enough research to have regulated guidelines for avoiding space junk. An imaginary rectangle is drawn around a given space vehicle on a mission. This 30-mile by 30-mile (48-km by 48-km) area is monitored, giving the team enough time to maneuver the debris if necessary. NASA's debris avoidance plan has been used successfully multiple times in the past decade.

CONTEMPORARY FINDINGS ON GRAVITY AND PLANETARY MOTION

Now that we're in the digital era, new technologies, ideas, and information enter the world every day. Because of the Internet and digitization, access to this information is also rapid.

Thus far, this century's work in understanding gravity and planetary motion has involved new discoveries that strengthen Einstein's ideas about relativity. Whether that's at the quantum level or in the vast expanse of the universe, the world has yet to find another thinker who can change the entire paradigm of how we understand and model the universe. Some findings are directly related to Einstein's predictions. One hundred years after presenting his gedankenexperiments, our technologies and scientists are able to prove that black holes and gravitational waves do exist and behave how Einstein's theories predicted they would.

Much of the research coming out of scientists and our leading institutions keeps technology at the forefront. This evolution is a result of digitization. From robotics to rockets, obtaining, storing, and disseminating information has never been easier. Many of NASA's efforts include the public and transparency. Imaging in particular, as championed by Hubble, continues to be a prolific source of qualitative and quantitative research for astronomers all over the world.

Gravitational Waves

A key prediction of Einstein's theory of general relativity was gravitational waves—or ripples along space-time that propagate as waves. It's hard to imagine this phenomenon. Consider what happens when you cannonball into a pool. Your body cuts through the water and drops toward the pool's bottom. On the surface of the water, there's a big splash closest to where your body encountered the top of the water. From that point of entry, your energy moves outward in ripples. Now imagine that the large mass is a collapsing star. The gravity radiating out of it as it dies causes a rippling along the fabric we know as space-time. Whenever an observer passes such a ripple, they'll observe space-time distorting.

In February 2016, scientists finally found evidence of gravitational waves. While they were able to demonstrate the existence of the waves before using detectors to try measuring distant, faint hints of such an instance, it wasn't until 2016 that proof came. Gravitational waves came to Earth from the distant universe. This first instance of gravitational waves resulted from the merger of two black holes. The merger of two black holes creates one massive, spinning black hole.

Though the merger of black holes has been predicted, it's never been observed. The closest we've now come is through the presence of these gravitational waves. This inability to

This image shows a pair of neutron stars orbiting each other very closely, causing gravitational waves to ripple along space-time.

visually observe the phenomena of distant space should be humbling. Like the scientists of the Scientific Revolution who could not see Earth or the rest of our solar system from outer space, we are at a moment in history where our technologies have not caught up with our ideas.

Two observatories with sophisticated laser detectors— Laser Interferometer Gravitational-wave Observatory (LIGO) detectors—identified the presence of gravitational waves. Both observatories are used to confirm the direction of the event causing the waves. Based on qualities of the detected waves, LIGO scientists have estimated that the black holes were about thirty times the mass of our sun. The event likely took place about one billion years ago.

Gravity, Orbiting Objects, and Planetary Motion

When two black holes orbit around each other, they lose energy. That energy is released in gravitational waves. Over a billion years, the black holes slowly move toward each other. Just like Einstein's famous equation $E = mc^2$ describes and proves, the energy turns into one huge mass when the two black holes eventually collide. The final release of energy from the collision is a huge burst of gravitational waves, which were detected by LIGO.

Prior to this moment, gravitational waves were only predicted to exist. In the 1970s and early 1980s, scientists discovered and observed a **binary system**. They noticed that the pulsar star orbiting around the neutron star kept shrinking as it released energy. This release, they predicted, was in gravitational waves. While the scientists did win the Nobel Prize for their findings, they only demonstrated that gravitational waves could exist—they did not have the technology to prove that existence.

LIGO's discovery is the first proof of gravitational waves themselves. Perhaps these waves will be our most visual representation of that ever-mysterious force, gravity, itself. It may seem small or mysterious, this discovery. It marks a new era in astronomic discovery. We are now pioneers of the warped side of the universe. These discoveries are like looking beneath the trampoline as the bowling ball stretches it. Hopefully, over time, we'll know what's the behind the curtain. Colliding black holes and gravitational waves are just the beginning of understanding what's on the warped side of space-time. Who knows what phenomena may present themselves next.

Pluto's Demotion When we learn about history, it often seems like the thinking of the past is unrecognizable compared to the information of the current generation. It seems crazy now to think that Earth was flat or that it was the center of the solar system.

But what used to be considered our ninth planet, Pluto, can help us keep perspective on how long it often takes to understand things. Pluto was observed and deemed the ninth planet in our solar system in 1930. Pluto's role as a planet only had a brief reign, though. Just a decade ago, it was determined that Pluto was, in fact, a **dwarf planet**. Like many things in science, the evidence was there all along. Since Pluto is very far away and it's substantially smaller than the eight other planets of our solar system, we might have guessed that it only *seems* like a planet.

Beyond Neptune, astronomers observed a ring of icy bodies. Today, these objects collectively are known as the Kuiper Belt. Upon closer examination, astronomer Mike Brown realized that one of the Kuiper Belt bodies was larger than Pluto. And so, in 2006, Pluto was demoted.

Pluto's demotion and the discovery of the Kuiper Belt brought in a whole new understanding about planetary motion and our model of the solar system. Now, astronomers

Gravity, Orbiting Objects, and Planetary Motion

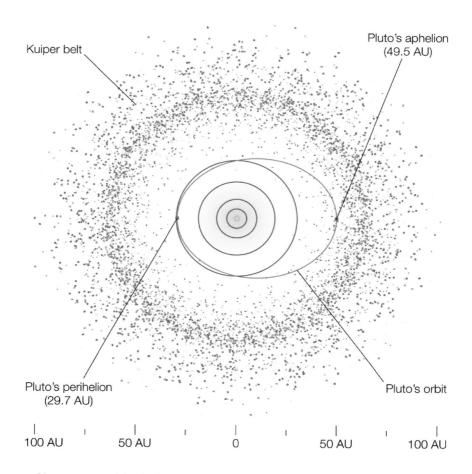

Kuiper belt

Pluto's aphelion
(49.5 AU)

Pluto's perihelion
(29.7 AU)

Pluto's orbit

| 100 AU | | 50 AU | | 0 | | 50 AU | | 100 AU |

Pluto was named for the Roman god of the underworld.

know that the outer reaches of our solar system are frigid
and contain many new, mysterious objects. As strange and
elusive as these objects may seem to us, the scientists who
discover them find them inspiring and rich with information
that could help us survive and thrive—and if not us, then the
universe at large. For example, some of these cold, distant

The Help of Hubble

The Hubble Space Telescope has been central to advancements in astronomy since its launch in the 1990s. From the mechanics and engineering of the telescope and the missions after its launch to fix and enhance it while in orbit, to the resulting images we've captured and stored, Hubble has championed a new world of astronomy entirely.

Hubble's images, taken by famous scientists and amateur astronomers, have paved the way for more than ten thousand scientific articles. While in some ways, we live in a time of increased secrecy, we also live during an era of decreased privacy in digital spaces. While there are many pros and cons to this way of life, one advantage is exemplified by Hubble's accessibility to the public—and not just the American public, but to any person of any nationality or age. Hubble's policies with regard to scholarship are a large reason why it has been so prolific to advancing astronomy. Many observatories have taken on this educational model, too.

An image taken by Hubble

bodies have drastically different densities from each other. The diversity of these bodies promises all kinds of discoveries.

The Universe Expanding

One prevailing idea of our understanding of the universe since Einstein's presentation of relativity is the big bang theory. Cosmologists like Stephen Hawking are interested in the creation of the universe. How and when did the universe start? Why? What was there before space? This field has grown since Einstein's work because space-time has offered scientists a new way of considering the inextricable link between time and space.

The big bang theory uses advancements in quantum physics along with relativity to offer a potential beginning of the universe. This theory predicts that the universe was born of a terrifically dense, hot point. The theory states that before the first second of the universe being born, inflation occurred, allowing space to expand faster than the speed of light. Again, if we think of the relationship between energy and mass, suddenly, we can imagine the universe growing from quanta to a tennis ball in an instant. In the beginning, there was matter—subatomic matter. As the universe slowly expanded and began to cool, this matter grew. The heat smashed atoms and broke them into dense plasma.

Cosmologists' understanding of the universe suggests that for the first few hundred thousand years, the universe was too

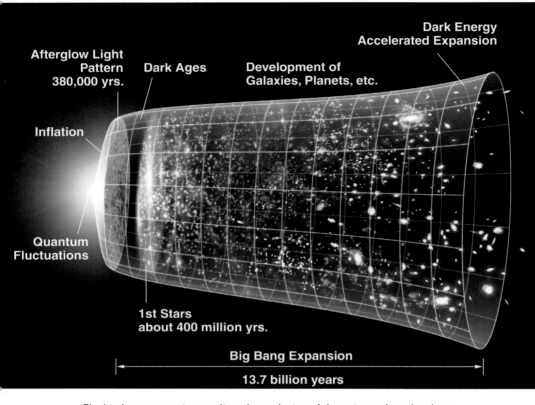

The big bang expansion predicts the evolution of the universe based on how light-years occur along space-time.

hot for light to shine. Afterward, matter cooled and the first flash of light was created. Like a streak of lightning, this flash resulted in a spell of darkness.

Four hundred million years later, the universe as we understand it emerged. Gas began to form stars. Stars gathered together to make galaxies. Galaxies produced light. Currently, scientists predict that the dark energy—a force we still don't quite understand—sped up the expansion of

Gravity, Orbiting Objects, and Planetary Motion

the universe. Nine billion years after the big bang, our solar system was born.

Ever since that big bang, space has stretched and carried matter with it. It's hard not to see this occurrence in a usual narrative way. After all, it seems like this moment is the beginning—the scientific version of "and God said, let there be light!" So far, the universe has been expanding for about thirteen billion years.

The astronomer to conceive of this theory that the universe was expanding was Edwin Hubble in the 1920s. It's no wonder, then, that our most important space telescope is called Hubble. One of the Hubble Space Telescope's important discoveries was an observation of a supernovae. In 1998, the image of the supernovae from Hubble proved that the universe was expanding more slowly than it is currently. Because we encounter gravity every moment of every day, we know it as a halting, heavy force. In the grand scheme of the universe though, gravity is not slowing things down. Scientists assume, for now, that dark energy is the next unknown force to find to understand the acceleration of the universe's expansion.

One huge mystery that the big bang leaves unsolved is the issue of shape. If the universe is expanding, what is it expanding into? Will expansion be infinite? Will the universe eventually reverse and head toward its subatomic state again? Finding and studying more space objects like dark energy and black holes will help us answer these sorts of questions. The key relationship is between gravity and expansion. The density of matter in the universe impacts the strength of gravitation. Gravitation and expansion counter each other.

One way to imagine this relationship is to think of a sphere. If the density of the universe exceeds a certain value (that value hasn't yet been named), then the universe is like a sphere's surface in how it curves and closes. Like a light cast along the surface, it will eventually reach its starting point. In this version, the universe has no end. But it's also not infinite—eventually, it will stop expanding and start to collapse. Scientists call this phenomenon the Big Crunch.

On the other hand, if the density of matter in the universe does not exceed that critical value, then space might be open and shaped like a saddle. In this version, the universe is boundless. Expansion will be infinite.

In a more recently believed version, the mass in the universe is equal to that critical density, unveiling a flat universe—as in a sheet of paper. In this version, the universe is also boundless. But the rate of expansion, in this case, could cause other phenomena that we can't yet conceive.

As much as it might seem that we know so much—so much more than the forefathers of science did in ancient Greece and the Scientific Revolution—our understanding of relativity and the wider universe illuminates just how much more observing and thinking we have left to do. In due time,

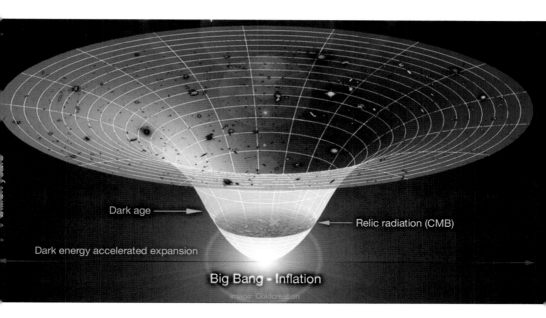

Dark age

Relic radiation (CMB)

Dark energy accelerated expansion

Big Bang - Inflation

Image: Coldcreation

Scientists believe that inflation and continued expansion—possibly infinite in nature—describe the universe's history and behavior.

our relationship to technology will continue to help us figure out the universe's mysteries. Like every generation before us, we are all destined to learn so much and leave our time with so many more questions.

Glossary

axis mundi The cosmic axis between heaven and Earth as represented by pillars, trees, and more in various philosophies and beliefs.

big bang The rapid expansion of matter from a state of high density and temperature, which scientists believe was the beginning of the universe; a theory that combines particle physics with astronomy.

binary system A system of two objects in space whose gravitational movement causes them to orbit around each other with and a central mass; usually made up of two stars orbiting each other.

cosmic rays High-energy radiation from outside of our solar system that can result in showers of particles that can penetrate Earth's atmosphere.

cosmography The branch of science that maps features of the universe. Cosmography includes astronomy, geography, and geology. Originally, the word indicated a description or visual representation of the universe or Earth.

cosmology The science of the origin and development of the universe, currently dominated by the big bang theory.

dark energy An unknown energy that scientists believe is present throughout space, causing the universe's expansion to accelerate.

early universe The portion of time encompassing the universe's initial inflation.

ellipse An oval shape traced by a point moving along a plane such that the sum of its distances from two foci is constant; the shape traced by planetary motion, especially according to Kepler, as proven by Newton.

extrasolar planets Planets that orbit stars other than the sun.

flat Earth theory Archaic models of Earth as shaped like a plane or disk, often floating in a larger ocean.

gamma ray burst Flashes of gamma rays emitted from high-energy explosions in space, as observed in distant galaxies; bright electromagnetic events lasting from ten minutes to several hours.

gedankenexperiment German for "thought-experiment"; a term claimed by Albert Einstein when describing his approach of using conceptual rather than actual experiments.

geocentrism A model of the universe in which Earth is depicted as the central body, based on former astronomical systems and predictions.

gravity A force that attracts a body toward any other body with a larger mass; from the Latin for "heavy" or "weight."

gravitational waves Ripples in the fabric of space-time predicted by Einstein.

heliocentrism A model of the universe in which the sun is depicted as the center of the universe, as in accepted astronomical models of our solar system.

interstellar dust The space between stars that is filled with atomic and molecular gas, particles, and dust; often appearing as a nebula.

inverse-square law A law in physics stating that a specified physical quantity or intensity in inversely proportional to the square of the distance from the source of that physical quantity.

orbital debris The growing collection of manmade objects or pieces of objects that are defunct but still orbiting Earth; also known as "space junk."

parallax The effect of an object appearing different based on the angle at which it is viewed.

precession The slow movement of the axis of a spinning body around another axis due to a torque, causing the direction of the first axis to change, as in Mercury's orbit around the sun.

relativity The dependence on the relative motion of an observer and observed objects by various physical phenomena regarding light, space, time, and gravity.

space-time The concepts of time and three-dimensional space placed into on four-dimensional continuum; the fabric along which physical phenomena in space occur.

solar wind A stream of energized particles flowing outward from the sun and through the solar system at very high speeds and temperatures.

space junk Defunct manmade objects still in space; known more formally as orbital debris.

telescope An optical instrument that uses precisely cut and arranged curved glass and mirrors to make distant objects seem nearer by magnifying them; from the Latin to see "at a distance," the first patent for a telescope belongs to Galileo.

terminator An astronomical term indicating the dividing line between light and dark on a given planetary body.

time dilation The difference of elapsed time between two events as measured by observers moving relative to each other.

universal gravitation Newton's law stating that two bodies attract each other with a force that is proportional to the product of their masses (and inversely proportional to the square of the distance between them).

Further Information

Books

Einstein, Albert, Hanoch Gutfreund, and Jürgen Renn. *Relativity: The Special & the General Theory: 100th Anniversary Edition*. Princeton, NJ: Princeton University Press, 2015.

Newton, Isaac, and Andrew Motte. *The Principia*. Amherst, NY: Prometheus Books, 1995.

Principe, Lawrence. *The Scientific Revolution: A Very Short Introduction*. United Kingdom: Oxford University Press, 2011.

Websites

Biography.com
http://www.biography.com
Biography.com captures the stories of famous people throughout history. This site features reading materials and documentaries about the central scientists in this book: Aristotle, Copernicus, Kepler, Galileo, Newton, Einstein, and Hawking.

HubbleSite

http://www.hubblesite.org/explore_astronomy/black_holes
This website allows people to explore black holes. The animation simulates real-time understanding of how black holes work. Using the same model as the Hubble Space Telescope, you can explore the virtual world of black holes.

The Physics Classroom

http://www.physicsclassroom.com
The Physics Classroom has information on the science behind the discoveries of the physicists. View models of how each of Newton's laws works with sample equations and descriptions.

Institutions

NASA

http://www.nasa.gov
NASA was developed in the late 1950s with hopes of leading the world in space exploration. From moon landings to satellites to rovers on Mars, NASA continues to make new discoveries all over the universe.

LIGO

http://www.ligo.caltech.edu
LIGO is the Laser Interferometer Gravitational-Wave Observatory. LIGO is supported by the National Science Foundation. It's operated by Caltech and MIT. LIGO confirmed the existence of gravitational waves in February 2016.

Bibliography

Choi, Charles Q. "Our Expanding Universe: Age, History & Other Facts." January 13, 2015. http://www.space.com/52-the-expanding-universe-from-the-big-bang-to-today.html

Dowling, Mike. "Aristotle's Conclusion." Retrieved May 9, 2016. http://www.mrdowling.com/601-aristotle.html

European Space Agency. "The Hipparcos Space Astrometry Mission." Retrieved May 13, 2016. http://www.cosmos.esa.int/web/hipparcos.

Harley, J. B., and David Woodward, eds. *The History of Cartography*. Vol. 1. Chicago: University of Chicago Press, 1987.

HubbleSite. "Hubble Essentials." Retrieved May 13, 2016. http://hubblesite.org/the_telescope/hubble_essentials.

Larson, Laurence Marcellus. *The King's Mirror: Translated from the Old Norwegian by Laurence Marcellus Larson*. New York: American-Scandinavian Foundation, 1917.

LIGO Lab. "Gravitational Waves Detected 100 Years After Einstein's Prediction." February 11, 2016. https://www.ligo.caltech.edu/news/ligo20160211.

NASA. "Ask an Astrophysicist: Stars." Retrieved May 12, 2016. http://imagine.gsfc.nasa.gov/ask_astro/stars.html.

——— . "Space Debris and Human Spacecraft." September 26, 2013. http://www.nasa.gov/mission_pages/station/news/ orbital_debris.html.

National Geographic. "Orbital Objects." Retrieved May 9, 2016. http://science.nationalgeographic.com/science/space/solar-system/orbital.

Practical Physics. "Greek Evidence for the Earth's Shape and Spin." Retrieved May 9, 2016. http://practicalphysics.org/ greek-evidence-earths-shape-and-spin.html.

Redd, Nola Taylor. "Black Holes: Facts." Space.com. Retrieved May 12, 2016. http://www.space.com/15421-black-holes-facts-formation-discovery-sdcmp.html.

Smithsonian's National Air and Space Museum. "Exploring the Planets." Retrieved May 13, 2016. https://airandspace.si.edu/ exhibitions/exploring-the-planets/online.

Tel Aviv University, Science and Technology Education Center. "Did Galileo Have Proof of the Earth's Movement?" Retrieved May 9, 2016. http://muse.tau.ac.il/museum/galileo/did_galileo.html.

Wall, Mike. "Five Years Later." Space.com. August 24, 2011. http://www.space.com/12709-pluto-dwarf-planet-decision-5-years-anniversary-iau.html.

Will, Clifford M. "Einstein's Relativity and Everyday Life." Physics Central: Learn How Your World Works. Retrieved May 10, 2016. http://physicscentral.com/explore/writers/will.cfm.

Index

Page numbers in **boldface** are illustrations. Entries in **boldface** are glossary terms.

About the Author

Lisa Hiton is a filmmaker and poet from Deerfield, Illinois. She first learned about the night sky from her father's telescope and reading Greek mythology. She went to film school at Boston University, where she learned about the practical physics of lighting. She's been traveling to Greece to write poems and make documentaries for the last few summers. She teaches film, poetry, literature, and education at universities on the East Coast.